THIS IS SHE

ISBN: 9798994549414
Published by: Alegria Publishing
Book cover and layout by: @mckadamia

THIS IS SHE

Ava Cázares

ALEgRÍA
PUBLISHING

To my Grandparents
A mis Abuelitos

This book contains poems that are written in both Spanish and English. Each poem originally written in Spanish is accompanied by a translation.

PREFACE

When I was a girl, a long brass mirror hung in the hallway of my childhood home, and in it, a stranger watched and waited. The first moment I laid eyes on her, my own glare sent goosebumps down my body and I covered my eyes, peaking between my fingers to see if I were still there.

I cannot say outright why I was startled by my own reflection; this is the mystery that is the first act of my life. Each time I looked at myself, squinting and gritting my baby teeth, the stranger looked as if she had something to say. I saw vulnerability and fragility in my own child eyes and I was intensely and entirely disturbed by it.

This phobia of mine at one moment subsided, then returned one day as I was sitting criss-cross in the soil of my grandmother's garden, picking and chewing on mint leaves. It had recently rained, and the damp and cool air became my first experience of an omen. Right at that moment, a single, heavy drop of water fell from the sky, making a 'plink' sound in a shallow puddle at my side. I leaned over curiously, stretching my neck out and sinking my hands into the soft mud. Once again, *there I was.* Those eyes of mine, my pursed lips, and the angst of my inescapable reflection.

I was an emotionally-hungry child with an internal harshness who felt seldom understood by others, but sought to understand everyone else. I often assaulted the adults around me with questions and kept notes on the people who stood in line for confession in Catholic mass. Long before I became a therapist, I practiced psychotherapy unethically on the swingset of my elementary school in a nearly trance-like state. I had no idea what I was doing, but I liked the sound of another child letting out a sigh after a long cry.

Admittedly, my softness and innocence are mourned by my rigid and stoic woman-self. I do not gasp or shutter in the mirror anymore, but there are times I sigh or furrow my brow. Sometimes, as a woman does, I feel ghostly and personless, succumbing to an inner void; other times, I am possessed, perhaps by all of the women in my bloodline at once. This is the very disharmony and deadness that unsettles me in the evening and the reason I am most restless. I am the detective, the suspect, and the red herring in my own mystery of the decade.

I have long found the phrase 'know thyself' to be the most haunting and cryptic threat ever made against me. At this age, I spit and curse at the 'know thyself', 'find oneself', and 'become oneself' evenly. When I was younger and more susceptible to these threats, I wrung every drop out of psychology, art, esoterism, and spirituality for some self-evidence that still left me parched. I have not been entirely unavailing, however; there are particular places I have seen myself that have left me feeling like I was right on the tip of my own tongue. The poetry of Alejandra Pizarnik, the female villains of the Mexican telenovelas of my childhood, the paintings of Remedios Varo, and the gut-wrenching ballads of Ana Gabriel are some of my most-frequented reflective surfaces and notable influences in my personhood.

My truest mirror, which must be mentioned, are the people who call me their therapist. I am young enough to remember the name and story of every patient I have ever had, an ability that one day I might lose to being 'seasoned'. My own traumas, fears, doubts, and ambitions have all sat in front of me at some point, almost mockingly, in a different body and voice. Each patient leaves my soul slightly changed for the wiser and each day at the hour mark, I am reminded I must take my own advice to look in the mirror.

After years of writing poetry, I am better-acquainted with myself than I once was. Perhaps this inner war was never about knowing, finding or becoming myself, but rather *remembering*. The question being asked is not 'who am I?' or 'who will I become?' but rather, 'who have I always been?'. Collecting my own poetry is to be my own historian and to whisper into these pages: *I am her and I have always been her.*

THIS IS SHE arrives in your hands during a timely and uncertain era. I have compiled nearly a decade of my poetry while enduring one of the most canonical experiences of womanhood— the quarter-life crisis. Here I fight against the amnesia-like nature of grief, pain, and angst, in a quiet and intimate storytelling of who I am. Wait for me, my beautiful reader, while I try to remember.

This is my recollection, my inventory of the soul, and my long, piercing stare into the mirror. **This is She.**

"*I don't know anything. Nothing fundamental. I don't know what I should have learned many years ago. Nobody taught me anything. I know, however, what I should know much later. Hence I feel like an old woman and a girl at the same time.*"

— Alejandra Pizarnik, *Diaries* (2004)

CONTENTS

ON
THE SELF

The Cold

I learned what a woman was
The day
I stayed home sick from school;
Laid
In my Mother's lap, faint and ill,
Never had I seen her this way before:
With one arm,
She pressed a cold cloth on my face;
With the other,
She nursed my baby brother;
When the telephone rang,
Her neck and third arm
Answered it,
And a voice
Through the cord tangled around her children
Spoke;
My Mother then,
Sitting up and clearing her throat,
Responded to the voice
With a string of words, so simple,
That would e c h o in my mind
For years to come—

"This is she,"

'It's a Girl'

A birth of eighteen hours, I held on for dear Death:
I unknotted the cord around my neck,
I made the sign of the cross, I braced my soul, and
I let out
A sigh in place
Of my first breath;

Nurture

I,
Being born of soil,
Am afraid of the sky;
Unlike a bird,
Fearless of what is beneath them— *A buried woman*
Fears the root beneath her;

To Be of Iron

This is how it feels
To be
      Of iron:
      Cold, hard, unbreakable;
      dense and invulnerable,
Wearing
The disguise of Woman;

Ser de Hierro

Así es como se siente
Ser
       De hierro:
       Fría, durísima, irrompible;
       densa e invulnerable,
Llevando
El disfraz de Mujer;

I Am Craving an Apple, Under an Orange Tree

He;
The most abundant, fruitful
And mature—
I eat his fruit
But I am starving—
  How,
   With the fruit of life,
Could man kill my hunger?

Se Me Antoja una Manzana, Debajo de un Naranjo

Él;

Lo más abundante, fructífero

Y maduro—

Como su fruta

Pero me muero de hambre—

     ¿Cómo,

     Con la fruta de vida,

Podría el hombre matar el hambre?

The Anvil

Once when I was an ant,
A herd of humans walked right over me as if I were
not there, nearly missing me, their steps casting
long shadows over my home in the crevice of the
sidewalk;
One of them picked me up on the underside of his
shoe,
Lifting me up high, (here I got to fly),
Then smeared me black, brown, and hot into the
pavement;
My Death went unnoticed and more herds went by,
Walking and living right over me—
As if I were not there at all;

THE PEOPLE-EATER

I only ate
What went well with the blood of my bitten
tongue
Till god gave me sense
To taste;
God's famine
Of two decades and one year
Was ended
By a curable hunger
Of a peculiar name

The Broom that Hardly Sweeps

The broom that hardly sweeps,
Has no reason to;
And until someone
Takes her out,
Here, she will stay
Dusty, idle and locked up
In the closet;

La Escoba que Menos Barre

La escoba que menos barre,
No tiene el para qué barrer;
Y hasta que alguien
La saque,
Aquí, quedará
Empolvada, ociosa y encerrada
En el clóset;

24th of September

What rivalry I have with my own birthday;
tomorrow, life will catch up to me in this rigged
race to Death,
Although last year, I nearly beat her;

The Inkblots

An angry woman bares
The reflection of her own face
      OR—
Two women,
A Mother and daughter nearly the same
Sit face to face,
Angered by their sameness;
That is,
If both interpretations
      Are at all
      Different

The Contents of My Purse

Pens I have taken from people
Perfume and playing cards
A lock without a key
A black mood ring
A polaroid of someone I do not know
An unopened letter from someone I do
A planchette
A single lavender tea bag, unsteeped
An embroidered 'A' handkerchief soiled with
lipstick
Clove chewing gum
My brasserie
One Mexican peso
A couple of journals; one full, one empty
Some nostalgia
A certain, very affecting childhood memory
A white lie
Three regrets
Two excuses; one real, one pretend
One deeply buried secret,
And a lighter for the women that smoke

'What Is It That You Do For A Living?'

'I clean' I say
I come
From a lineage of women
Who cleaned;
There they are, kneeling on the floor
Of other families' homes
With their rag and bucket,
Scrubbing away at spots and messes
They did not make;
Here I am, standing
In a noisy, dirty world,
My ears wide,
Listening
And scrubbing away
At spots and messes I did not make—
'I'm a therapist'

The Daughter and Her Shoulders

I was born with shelves for shoulders,
Made to carry;

On the left, I carry:
Family sins, ghosts of the past,
And many ill-fitting masks;
A wicked nostalgia,
A very deep void,
Someone's belongings they do not want back,
And everything heavy
Holding me back

    On the right, I keep
    The will
    To forget it all— the only thing
Without weight
Holding me up

La Hija y Sus Hombros

Nací con estantes por hombros,
Ya puestos para cargar;

En el izquierdo, cargo:
Pecados familiares, fantasmas del pasado,
Y máscaras que no me quedan;
La maldita nostalgia,
Un hueco profundísimo,
Las pertenencias de alguien que no quiere recuperar,
Y todo lo pesado
Que me detiene;

      En el derecho, guardo
      La gana
      De olvidarlo todo— el único
Sin peso
Que me sostiene

My Mind's Creation

Last night I dreamt I was a Mother—
My baby
Latched to me,
Her firsts unclenching
And cupping
What is
Her never-shallow chalice;
My baby,
Sinless; Fed; and Forgiving,
Took communion
From her Mother's thirsting soul;

A Yearning

What I am missing
I cannot remember
I only know
I lack it;
Where I belong
I cannot remember,
I only know
I must not
Be home;

Distance

I am not afraid that I am incapable—
I am afraid that I am powerful
And perhaps,
That power
Is hiding from me, someplace
Between the dead-end street on which I live
And the pink walls of this room;

I do not know where it hides;
I only hope
That when I find it,
It does not tell me
That *I* am the one
In hiding

Lejanía

No tengo miedo de que soy incapaz—
Tengo miedo de que soy poderosa
Y quizás,
Ese poder
Está escondiéndose de mí, en algún lugar
Entre la calle sin salida en que vivo
Y las paredes rosas de esta habitación;

No sé dónde se esconde;
Solo espero
Que cuando lo encuentre,
Que no me diga
Que la que se esconde
Soy *yo*

The Understudy

I do not know of
This woman I am—
I see her;
She is an apparition,
Appearing, vanishing,
And reappearing before me,
Strobing the blue light of the moon; I reach for
her,
Ghostly, womanly overcoat,
But my hands only clasp dryly in the air,
For she is only,   *A projection;*

ON LOVE

Forbidden Fruit

Man,

The Colonizer

Of my Eden, comes unhungry and prances away

With a throat-full; Man, the greedy, the

unknowing in fig-leaf,

Leaves this tree entirely bare;

Now I, *a native*, must hide

A certain fruit

Of my sustenance–– and eat it only

While he is East

Suffocation of Sight

When I first caught the eyes of a woman,
I felt as though I could not breathe;
My eyes,
Nearly blind,
Were stolen by hers for sight;
Her eyes,
Gripping onto mine Sternly; Softly; Selfishly,
Would not unhand me;
They drowned me deeply,
Without breath and without sound
For what seemed like the lifetime
Of someone much older than I;
Then like nothing,
She let go———— She dropped me
In this unconcerned, fleeting entrancement
That reminded me of a kind of theater;

The Shadow

Selfish light, *prudish blindfold,*
I see why you hide from me
What you do;
You fear I may leave you
For the night;
Dark mistress, shapely void—
You cast on my wall,
          Arched, like a cat
Against a waning moonlight;
Lady of light, yes,
Be afraid

My Land, Unconquerable

Visitor, Tourist, Nomad, Vagabond,
Come and see my land—

Here is The Hill;
To your right,
The road and my sunken steps,
Some wet and some dry;
  Follow them and see if you can climb what is mine

Terreno Mío, Inconquistable

Visitante, Turista, Nómada, Vagabunda,
Que venga y que vea mi tierra—

Aquí está La Colina;
A su derecha,
El camino y mis pasos hundidos,
Algunos mojados y otros secos;
Que los siga y a ver si usted puede escalar lo mío

Eternal January

The sun has not yet returned
And the day remains dark;

Rain droplets
Paint the window
And behind their fog,
I think
I see your face— emotionless, cold, as you are;
But when the weight of the drops
Makes them fall
down
   the
        glass— *it looks as though you are crying*
        for me;
The first
And the only time
You would have done so;

Enero Eterno

El sol todavía no ha vuelto
Y el día se queda oscuro;

Las gotitas de lluvia
Pintan la ventana
Y detrás de su niebla,
Creo
Que veo tu rostro— sin emoción, frío, como eres;
Pero cuando el peso de las gotas
Las hace caer
por
   el
        cristal— *parece que estás llorando*
        por mi;
La primera
Y la única vez
Que lo hubieras hecho;

Insuperable Restlessness

Cruel bed,
I do not know you;
If I am eternally sick—
At least,
Let me rot
In the bed of the person
Who infected me

Inquietud Insuperable

Cama cruel,

No te conozco;

Si estoy eternamente enferma—

Al menos,

Déjame pudrirme

En la cama de la persona

Que me contagió

You Were, You Are and You Will Be

You are
The only being
Immune from my chasm;
Who because of your immensity—you cannot fall;
You remain detached
From the face of my planet—
Suspending me in the air, *so that I do not jump,*
Like the king of Here
And of;
The Beyond

Fuiste, Eres y Serás

Eres

El único ser

Inmune de la sima mía;

Que por tu inmensidad—no puedes caer;

Permaneces desapegado

De la faz de mi planeta—

Suspendiéndome en el aire, *para que yo no salte,*

Como el rey de Aquí

Y de;

Lo *Más Allá*

The Shape of a Guitar

The hips
W i d e and grippable
Like the shape of a guitar,
Do not play on their own;
But suddenly—
Sat in your lap,
You grab her
And she whispers to you,
"Touch me" / "Play me"

La Forma de una Guitarra

Las caderas

A n c h a s y agarrables

Como la forma de una guitarra,

No tocan solitas;

Pero de repente—

Sentada en tu regazo,

La agarras

Y te murmura,

"Tócame"

Mrs. Juana

One hot afternoon,
A woman dressed like a man
Made me
Sweat
Seeing her in her suit;
Chivalrous,
She gave me her handkerchief
For the sweat
And apologized
For making me wet

Doña Juana

Una tarde calurosa,
Una mujer vestida de hombre
Me hizo
Sudar
A verla en su traje;
Caballerosa,
Me sacó su pañuelo
Para el sudor
Y me pidió perdón
Por hacerme mojada

This, Is My Nearness To You

My love,
My mind
Will not rest with you in it;
My solitude
Will not escape
The scalloped edges
Of your ubiquity;
Of the things
I wish
I could get away with
And get away from—
My love,
You are not one

"Unsex Me Here"

I trade in
Our alikeness, our mirror-like love
For each other;
Handlessness, sexlessness; our love unlaid and
unallowed,
If I cannot lay
A hand, a head, or lips on you,
Then let me lay and dress
My eyes
In the demoralizing disguise
Of man

The Forest of Chapultepec

If I were truly a bird, I would fly over the forest;
The light mist against the air, streaming down my
face,
Not knowing if it were tears or rain;
Female downpour,
I would rain upon my man of the land below,
As his weeping lover / sky;

El Bosque de Chapultepec

Si yo realmente fuera un pájaro, yo volaría sobre el
bosque;
La ligera niebla contra el aire, corriendo por mi
cara,
Sin saber si fueran lágrimas o lluvia;
El aguacero femenino,
Yo llovería sobre mi hombre de la tierra de abajo,
Como su cielo llorón;

Hiding

You put the universe in disorder, distancing yourself
from me!

You insulted
All that is Divine!
You acted against the law
That keeps the sun and the moon together— *we are*
not together!

The sun that one day awakened me,
Wants to burn me;
And the moon that one night consoled me,
Hides
As I do

Escondiéndome

¡Pusiste el universo en desorden, *distanciándote de mí!*

¡Insultaste
A todo Divino!
Actuaste en contra de la ley
Que mantiene el sol y la luna juntos— *¡juntas, no estamos!*

El sol que un día me despertó,
Quiere quemarme;
Y la luna que una noche me consoló,
Se pone escondida
Igual que yo

To 'Gatsby' Oneself

What have I gained
From this tragic flaw?
I gained
Only an idea of a god— its pedestal, always
occupied;
Sore, bruised knees,
And a means to obscure
My own
Colorlessness;

Catherine Linton

In your cold absence,
I am Nowhere,
      Noplace,
      Noone;
Spine of my back, Dowel of my core:
You were, in your singleness, the sameness
Of two souls;
You were everything— I am a nothingness, *much
colder*

A Homebody

Sometimes when I wash the dishes,
I remember—
My former self
Who loved a man completely

Sometimes I wonder
What it would feel like
To remove a ring before I wash the dishes,
Fear scratching it on a glass,
Or losing it down the drain;
I pretend
He is behind me in the kitchen,
Cleaning up after dinner,
Helping me do half
Of what makes a home;
I hear him
> *Over the sound of the faucet;*
He tells our child he will be up in a minute;
> *I feel him*
Kiss me on my cheek;

Sometimes then—
The water turns as cold as the truth—
It splashes me in the face,
I pause
And turn to find
A homeless house and a deafening silence
Behind me;
I finish the dishes with my empty left hand,
I turn down the lights of my kitchen,
I clear my throat,
And I whisper *'goodnight'*
To a reality
That has betrayed me;

Her Father

Deep; buried and red
A tenderness
Of insurmountable and inborn sort swells within

Becoming; nestled, warm,
Beneath my cold ignorance of nature—
My baby unborn
Breathes and sleeps,
Rests,
And *reaches*
Through my gifted rib— for the love this man gives
Her Mother

It Is in These Moments that
I Think of You

It is in these moments
That I think of you—

I think of you:
When cold air seeps through my window
When I hear the first few pitter-patters of rain on
this roof
When the time changes,
And when I pour milk into my coffee;
I think of you:
When I hear the chord of A minor
When the lights come on after the film and it is
time to leave
When I look at paintings
When I cannot sleep
When I cry
When I write
When I stutter
When I sin
When I finish the last page of a book
And mostly,
When I try not to

How Do You Know If a Door Is Real?

This door is only a thought,
Knockable / touchable,
Like me;
If you knock / touch,
This bastard son of a tree—
Obstructing and thoughtful,
Will open wide
At last

¿Cómo Sabes Si una Puerta Es Real?

Esta puerta es solo un pensamiento,
Tocable,
Como yo;
Si la tocas,
Este bastardo hijo de árbol—
Estorbado y pensativo,
Se abrirá de par en par
Por fin

The Swallow

We are distant: the love between a swallow and a
human;
I fly away from you and I return, you move away
from me and you come close;
      Distant,
Like the eyebrows of Frida

La Golondrina

Distantes, somos: el amor entre una golondrina y
un humano;
Vuelo lejos de ti y vuelvo, te alejas de mi y te
acercas;
      Distantes,
Como las cejas de Frida

We, The Nocturnal

The Day has eyes
But he cannot see; *He*
Only sees me after dusk

Nosotros, Los Nocturnos

El Día tiene ojos
Pero no puede ver; *Él*
Solo me mira en el anochecer

The Third Act

You and I,
The unconvincing story;
This act
Of not loving each other, has only made me love
you more;
This disguise so seductive,
Has fused with my skin
And now,
I cannot discern
Which side of the curtain I am on

El Tercer Acto

Tú y yo, la novela
Poco convincente;
Este acto
De no amarnos, solo me ha hecho amarte más;
Este disfraz tan seductivo,
Se ha fusionado con mi piel
Y ahora,
No puedo discernir
En cuál lado de la cortina estoy

Interlude on Love & Anger

I.

Love
Introduced me to Anger;
A beautiful emotion with two lines between her brows;
Once when I was in bed,
Anger broke down the door of my bedroom
After I would not let her in;
She yelled at me to *feel* her:

     "But I am not an angry woman,"
I contested,
     "I do not have it in me"
"You do not have it in you?" Anger scoffed

Anger shrugged
And gestured behind her
To my eight-year-old self
Standing in the doorway
...

Anger spoke,

"Are you sure?"

II.

I then became what I had never been,
A red-eyed, green-faced woman-like god,
Possessed for the first time
With human E M O T I O N...

III.

I let out
A long scream; my mouth is a warhorn;

Anger told me to keep going—
I did:
I broke the bones of the planet's axis
I crushed them into my palms
I rubbed the dust into my hair;
I tore through the sky
I killed Orion in front of his Mother
I wrote my name in his blood between my breasts;
Anger became afraid, she retreated to the corner;
I kept going—
I bit into the appendages of an unimposing god
I spit the pulp back into his face;
I scared the devil into prayer;
I ravaged through everything and everyone that
moved;

Anger screamed at me to stop!
She put her hands on me, she tried to cover my mouth,
She got in my way—
I choked the sound out of Anger's throat
For raising her voice to me,
I hog-tied her limbs, raising her up to eclipse the
sun,
I made her beg me for mercy
And then when she did—
I dropped her limp body in the name of sin
        And I told Sin to commit me;

IV.

When Anger came to,
        She was not angry with me;
                She only cleared her voice softly,
Moving her hair from her face,
And asked,

                        "Are you through?"

V.

When I was through,
Anger introduced me to Despair,
A beautiful emotion with a perpetual tear-stained face;
Despair threw herself onto my lap, childlike:
"Lay and weep!" she cried
"Cry, cry until the sea becomes of it!"

VI.

With Despair, I wept;
The only woman who has ever heard my whimper;

I waded with her
In a cold sea of my own making,
So long,
My swollen eyes, now red, could hardly open
And my skin, turned blue, was now numb;

I whispered to Despair as her face slowly sank
under the water,
"I think it is time for me to go"

VII.

Suddenly, I awoke
On the beach of tragedy;

When I opened my eyes,
A stone-faced woman
Who called herself Redemption,
Appeared above me, hands on her hips;

"Stand up" Redemption said

Before I could,
Redemption dragged me up by the arm and ear;
She dusted me off
And said to me,
Quite sternly,
                    "Enough"

VIII.

There on the beach,
Anger, Despair & Redemption
  All stood before me;

  Anger told me to never deny myself of her,
  Despair reminded me to always *feel*,
And Redemption—
Redemption simply opened my palms,
And in them, she placed
Paper and pen;

The End.

MOUTHY

The wise idiot who said that talk is cheap
Was not a poet;
The idiot poet who wrote this for you
Was not me

BOCONA

El idiota sabia que dijo que hablar es barato
No era poeta;
El idiota poeta que te escribió esto
No fui yo

The Drunken Philosopher

The fifth shot
Of Mezcal
Tastes like *woman;*
A taste which before this,
Seemed extinct

La Filósofa Borracha

El fondo blanco
Del Mezcalito quinto
Lleva un sabor de *mujer*
Que antes,
Me parecía extinto

Helena

*H*im:
*H*umorous, *h*eart-*h*aving, *h*and-*h*olding, *h*andsome;
*H*owever—
*H*e's *h*ardly *H*er

Ritualistic Idiocy

Each morning
I dunk my tea bag in boiling water
Seven times;
Thrice to represent the three people I have loved
Twice more for the two for whom I only lusted
Once for *you*, who is reading this now

And once more for old time's sake

I Like Red Ones

When you asked me
What color flowers I liked,
I lied;
I do not like pink—
Nor is my life that color,
>   *Although I would like it to be*

Red suits me better
Because it reminds me of blood and my guts,
And the animals, whose bodies
Hang from hooks at the butcher;
Although I would never tell you this
Because I do not want you to think I am that
intense,
That morbid,
>   *Although I am;*
Nor did I want to obligate you to buy me flowers
>   *Although I did want them*
>   *{And I still want them}*
But thank you very much for this pink bouquet,
They are beautiful;

Me Gustan Las Rojas

Cuando me preguntaste
Qué color de flores me gustaba,
Mentí;
A mí no me gusta la rosa—
Tampoco vivo esa vida pintada,
Aunque quisiera

Me queda mejor el rojo
Porque me recuerda de sangre y mis entrañas,
Y los animales, cuyos cuerpos
Cuelgan de ganchos en el carnicero;
Aunque nunca te diría esto
Porque no quiero que pienses que soy tan intensa,
Tan morbosa,
Aunque sí soy;
Que tampoco quería obligarte a comprarme flores
Aunque sí las quería
{Y las quiero}
Pero muchísimas gracias por este ramo rosita,
Son hermosas

April 11th

Look—
How her sun *shines* without covering itself up
Smell—
How her sweet and fragrant flowers *bloom* without
withering
Listen—
How her little birds sing without interruption;
Plentiful, peaceful,
The Springtime is;
Now, imagine if she had a boyfriend;

Abril, 11

Miren—

Como su sol *brilla* sin taparse

Huelan—

Como sus flores dulces y perfumadas *florecen* sin
marchitarse

Escuchen—

Como sus pajaritos cantan sin interrupción;

Plena, pacífica,

Es la Primavera;

Ahora, imagínense si tuviera novio;

Pisces

The blue and cool
Man who loves me
Waits
Beside me
With a bucket of water

The hot, red
Fury in my cheeks
      Ignites
As the man,
His love, and his bucket,
Disarm me *gently,*
Like an endearing inconsequence
Of man's discovery
Of
Fire

When Time Resumes

In years from now
I might think of you in my sleep

When I roll onto my side,
My hand might reach behind me
To make sure you are not there;
Then later,
Once I wake up completely,
I might ask myself *why* you are not

I might then glance at the telephone

I might call you,
  It might ring,
I might motion to hang up
And then suddenly—
I might hear,
The soft buzz begin on the other line;
...
I might hold my breath
In an insufferable silence,

  ...
I might then
Hear your lips open to speak— Then,
And only then,
Might the clock beside my bed return to ticking;

ON THE BODY

The Fever

"One hundred and one, one hundred and two",
Two nuns chant at my bedside as my fever climbs
"One hundred and three"
And their voices become louder,
One of them holds an hourglass in her hands,
I squint through the sweat dripping into my eyes
But I cannot see how much time I have left;
The other,
Holds a small bag of sand behind her back
But I cannot exactly say if I am worthy

Eleven-Years-Old

I got my period for the very first time
On a trampoline;
One moment I was a girl—
Jumping and doing cartwheels;
Only a moment later,
There were gushes of blood
Pouring from me;
Gushes and gushes
Dripping down the unshaved legs of a child,
Soaking through
The white lace socks I was gifted for my
communion;
...
What have I done to myself? I thought
...

I crawled to the grass,
Holding with my hands
What I thought was a wound;
I bowed over it
And I prayed:
Am I dying, god?
Have I done something wrong?
I am so sorry, god
Please do not let me die;
I promise, I will be good;

My Mother found me there, legs-clenched in the
grass;
She told me,
I was not dying—
I was just becoming a woman
And now it was time to go inside

Life, In The Dichotomy
of Disgust & Desire

When I was eleven,
Boys wrinkled their noses at me, pretending to gag
Because my hips grew apart
And my breasts came in before anyone else's;

When I was sixteen,
The same boys moaned and thrusted at me in
laughter,
Whistling when I walked by— (now they like me)—
The same boys
Later grew into 'men'
Who now wag their fingers at me, warning me
That I better take care of myself
Because I will not be any good
Past twenty-two

Anti-Nature

I arrange the world, religion, laws, institutions, for my self-importance; I am willing to die— disposably in wars, if it means I am strong or brave; I will grapple and wound you for sport, if it means I am a winner; I lay down— liberally, undiscriminating, if it means I am 'wanted'; I shout and lecture, if it means someone will hear me, believe in me; I bulk and broaden, if it means someone will notice me; I fight against an *Innate* power by inventing my own—— *who do I sound like?*

The Breast Mouse

The breast mouse lives in my chest
In the unit above
The polyps and cysts on the bottom floor;
She,
My oldest tenant,
Is quiet and harmless
Unlike
Other vagrants and pests
Who squat
And ransack as they please;
She,
Unlike most,
Is the best company
My body has had
In some time

The Pill

Pill,

  How might I not be tempted
  By the purple-eyed,
Lock-jawed Mothers,
Wipers
And Tasters of their own snot
And tears?
  How,
  If at all,
  Might I thank you
  For the time you have spared me
  In years?

The Hair Is The Preface To The Mind

When I was girl
My hair was so long,
People who I did not know
Would touch it without asking;
     Once,
An older man behind me at the supermarket
     Stroked my hair all the way down my
backside;
     I shuddered in fear from his touch
As my Mother, smacked his hand from my head
And scolded him
Louder than I had ever heard her yell;

I was only seven-years-old
And in my child mind,
I convinced myself that this man,
From having touched my head,
Could now read my every thought;
From then on,
I tucked it in the sleeve of my sweater in case
anyone else tried to read my mind,
And eventually,
I cut it off altogether, to protect myself from
unwanted touch;
This may be why
I fell in love with the first person
To run their fingers through my thoughts
With my permission;

Purgatory

In purgatory
Women wear hospital gowns;
        One woman,
        Loudly-spoken,
        Is saying the rosary
        Now for the second time;
        A second woman,
        Is a new Mother
        In the past tense,
        She is entirely silent;
        Then there is me—
        I am the third woman
        Writing a poem-;
        The only way to kill time
        Before my body kills me

Womanhood in Parallel

The blood finally bled
On a cold chair beside the doctor;
My head fell back in relief,
And I began to cry
When suddenly— another cry, down the hall;
This cry
Was unlike mine;
It was a shriek that stiffened the hair on my neck;
It roared
It howled and heaved
Like an animal,
Like something I had never heard before,
Something primal,
Something
My body recognized before my mind;
Someplace deep, deep,
Buried in my body,
Even there, with my empty womb,
I could just feel,
I just knew ——— A Mother had lost her baby;

Interlude on Age

The Gut

My once-scarce self,
Rid
And infantile,
Was raised by an elder;
     Mother
Of my emptiness,
Surrogate
To the intuition
That took its place

The Taste of Wisdom

Give me, Give me
The cheekbones of an older woman
Give me her eyes
Prophets, who see
Give me her mouth, red, full
Of words,
And give them to me;
Give me everything
      She knows; and *give me,*   *She,*
Who tastes of wisdom

Lip Parentheses

Eleven times
My eyes slipped;
Speechless,
My eyes said
To let them drown
Down there;
And when I fought to keep them up,
They laid;
They made
Up a bed in a warm place, down where
It was safe
To sleep,
To surrender
Their sight

Ava Cázares

Salt & Pepper

At dinner,
There was a woman
Leaning across the table
With a head of gray

Her gray—
Reminded me of the way
The sky warns us of a storm;
I thought maybe one day,
Lightning had struck her
And had left her silver;
Or maybe,
This was where the light of the moon
Came from;
The head of the woman
Across the table
Held it

Though I sat far from her, a head of dark brown
On the other side of age,
I met eyes to tell her
      I should have just told her
That her hair
Brought the sky indoors

The End.

ON THE SPIRIT

Persephone's Return

I awaken each year in September
From a months-long sleep—
A cool wind and the smell of firewood
Leak through the center split
Of this mind,
Kindly
Reminding me
To think;
A flock
Of crows with familiar voices
Arrive and crowd
Outside the two windows
Of the face,
Cawing
Cackling
Pecking at the pupil,
Cruelly
Reminding
Me
To
See

My House-Elf Told Me,

He wants me to go out

He told me
That I should not hide
Nor stay here with him
Locked up,
Waiting for someone to take me
Outside;
He took me by the hand
And he himself opened the door for me;
There in the doorway, for the first time,
The softness of the wind
Caressed my face;
He showed me the warm, provoking light,
Known to put color on one's skin;
He took three steps ahead of me
And gestured:

He tells me
That now,
All I have to do
Is come out

El Duende de Mi Casa Me Dijo,

Que quiere que yo salga

Me dijo
Que no me debería esconder,
Ni quedarme aquí con él
Encerrada,
Esperando que alguien me acompañe
Afuera;
Me tomó de la mano
Y él mismo me abrió la puerta;
Allí en la entrada, por primera vez,
La suavidad del viento
Acarició mi cara;
Me mostró la luz, cálida y provocadora,
Conocida por poner color en la piel;
Dio tres pasos delante de mí
Y me hizo un gesto:

Me dice él
Que ahora,
Todo lo que tengo que hacer
Es salir

Last Night I Dreamt,

That god was a waiter;
He didn't say anything, he just came to the table
and I told him what I wanted;
Then he brought me all the wrong dishes,
disgusting, repulsive, and nothing of what I
wanted;
An old lady at my side whispered in my ear,
"look at him and look at him well!"
I looked at him and this time differently,
I saw that the sides of his head were flat and he
didn't even have ears to hear;

Anoche Soñé,

Que dios era mesero;
No dijo nada, solo acercaba a la mesa y le di mi
pedido;
Luego me trajo todos los platos equivocados, ascos,
repulsivos, nada que quería;
Una viejita a mi lado me susurró al oído,
"¡míralo y míralo bien!"
Lo miré y esta vez diferente,
Vi que los lados de su cabeza eran planos y ni tuvo
orejas para escuchar;

Blasphemy

I made the neighborhood happy
The day I silenced a man;

I cut his tongue out
And I threw it
At the hungry birds on the corner;
I then cut out his vocal chords, one by o n e,
And I gave some to the neighbor who always
wanted to sing;
The rest—
Well, I split them between the silent girls of the
neighborhood;
Today when I heard
Their yells and complaints for the first time,
That,
Made *me* happy

Blasfemia

Puse contento el vecindario
El día que silencié a un hombre;

Le corté la lengua
Y la eché
A los pájaros hambrientos de la esquina;
Luego le corté sus cuerdas, una por u n a,
Y le regalé unas a la vecina que siempre quería
cantar;
El resto—
Pues, se las dispersé a las chicas silenciadas del
barrio;
Hoy cuando escuché
Sus gritos y sus quejas por primera vez,
Eso,
Me puso *a mí* contenta

Pride & Wrath

If god, nor the government, nor his Mother
Have any punishment for this man, *I have*
A black candle, ground chili, and my own voice;

Orgullo e Ira

Si dios, ni el gobierno, ni su Madre
Tiene castigo por este hombre, *yo tengo*
Una vela negra, chile molido, y mi propia voz;

Gluttony, Sloth & Lust

What separates cloth and body
In this bed,
If not a straddling god
Lowering his gaze at who I am,
And who I am about to
Commit?

To the Woman Who Tried to Curse Me:

In the whites of the egg
In this glass of water,
There you were

You appeared
In all of your unsightliness:
Contorting;
Clawing; clinging;
        And there you went ...
Whisking;
Whining; writhing; and weaning from me
Like the bastardized daughter of a beast,
Unloved by its Mother

The Butcher

I did not steal his heart
For love;
I stole it for soup

But I discovered
He must not have loved anyone:
When I tasted it, it was horrible;
I offered it
To a limping woman with a tin can
And she cursed at me— she did not want it;
Then I tried to give it
To the bony dog on the street, *and without smelling it,*
He threw it back on
     the
         ground;

La Carnicería

No robé su corazón
Por amor;
Lo robé por caldo

Pero descubrí
Que él no debe haber amado a nadie:
Cuando lo probé, era horrible;
Se lo ofrecí
A una mujer coja con una lata
Y me maldijo— no lo quiso;
Luego traté de darle
Al perro huesudo de la calle, *y sin olerlo,*
Lo tiró en

    el

        piso;

The Ghost Who Lived Here Before Me

Tells me
I am dead: An unmarried, purple-eyed,
melancholic young woman, moping room to room,
entirely reflectionless;

I tell her with full breath in my chest:
"My unmarriedness is how I know I am,
In fact,
Not"

What Happened at Ladies' Pond

At Ladies' Pond,
The place of the unbaptism,
I became unsinned

I became *bodiless*
As I was
Before the body was to become
The place of baptism
For boys and men;
I became again
Therein in the water;
The first time I *became,*
Since last
I *f l o a t e d*
Inside of my Mother

The Boogieman

Right about to eat,
The Boogieman inside me
Took away my appetite;
He put fear in my mind
And stomach
That I am not going to be anyone in this life;
Or worse,
That I will be nobody with noone, and nothing
To eat
But I shut him up,
And I ate some bread
To shake off the fear

El Cucuy

Justo a punto de comer,
El Cucuy que llevo adentro
Me quitó el apetito;
Me puso miedo en la mente
Y el estómago
Que no voy a ser nadie en esta vida;
O peor,
Que voy a ser nadie sin nadie, con nada
De comer
Pero lo callé,
Y me comí mi bolillo
Para quitarme del susto

The Eighth Circle

When two clouds in the sky parted--
I came out;
I stepped out
With one bare foot
Planted firmly in the damp Earth,
Eyes wide;

In the thick and filthy air,
I saw
Several things that scared me:
Devils with wings and people with horns,
   Snakes and other animals procreating in
the street,
Screams from the other side
And the sobbing of someone near but hidden;
No one
Greeted me, or even saw me,
They all simply carried on without me
In their little hell;
Hence,
I retired;

El Octavo Círculo

Cuando dos nubes en el cielo se separaron––
Salí;
Pasé
Con un pie descalzo afuera
Plantado firme en la tierra húmeda,
Con los ojos anchos;

En el aire grueso y sucio,
Vi
Varias cosas que me asustaron:
Diablos con alas y personas con cuernos,
   Serpientes y otros animales procreando en
la calle,
Gritos del otro lado
Y el sollozo de alguien cercano pero escondido;
Nadie de allí
Me saludó, ni me vio,
Solo andaban sin mi
En su infierno pequeño;
Así que,
Me *retiré*;

THE STAIN

My lipstick left
A red stain
On the communion cup— The priest came close to
the boy
And did the same to his heart;

LA MANCHA

Mi labial dejó
Una mancha roja
En la copa de comunión— El padre se acercó al
niño
E hizo lo mismo con su corazón;

Metanoia

This clothing
Disguises
The nudity of my mind;
This closet
Makes a reliquary
Of my holy
And h o l l o w body;

Does God Have Favorites?

God, all-good,
Is it godly of you
To feed some
And
Starve others?... "Everyone, let us say grace"

Woman-fearing

The Moon is my girlfriend
And Venus,
My wife;
The Earth is my Mother
The Universe,
My godMother;
And You—
You;
Are the first version of a god
That I recognize

Sometimes Death

Between melting
Drowning
Burning
Falling
Jumping
Starving
And the sickness
Of holding onto my own secrets;
I chose a death
That is *a l i v e*;
   I choose a death
That is walking
Breathing
Hiding
Wasting
And w e a r a b l e;

Holy Thursday

Heart of cobwebs, bony soul;
Clean mind,
Dry eyes, empty arms— I had to give you up for
Lent, my love;

El Jueves Santo

Corazón de telarañas, alma huesudo;
Mente limpia,
Ojitos secos, brazos vacíos— te tuve que dejar por
Cuaresma, mi amor;

The Hanged Man

While she makes me coffee,
I ask the lady why
What I have always leaves me

To have something,
You have to let it go, she says

But Ma'am,
If I let him go, I will lose him

She responds:
You cannot lose what you do not have;
Let him go,
And he will be yours

El Colgado

Mientras me hace café,
Le pregunto a la señora por qué
Lo que tengo siempre se me va

Para tener,
Hay que soltar, me dice

Pero Señora,
Si lo suelto, lo perderé

Me contesta:
No puedes perder lo que no tienes;
Suéltalo,
Y será tuyo

Warning

On the other side of a condensated window,
Out in the misty cold,
Up in the dense, green hardwood,
Atop a flimsy, non-promising branch:
An owl *coos* in the syllables of your name

Sagittarius Archery

A single arrow
Spears me between the breasts;

I fall far
From the cloud upon which I sat;
Through the firmament, fog and trees,
Past the birds and trumpets,
And I land, triumphantly
On your lap;
You wash
The blue of the sky out of my eyes,
You fill them with the brown of soil;
You suspend my wings
And grow me roots,
You teach me not
To fly away
But to *walk*
With feet and flaw;

When I Almost Met Death

Skinny death,
The night is so dark;
I kneel before you
At the chosen hour;
Skinny death,
Comfort me
Care for me
Heal me
Take me

"No.

No, my daughter;
Sit before my bony feet,
Lie beneath my black cloak;
I will comfort you
I will care for you
I will heal you
But no,
I will not take you;

What does not kill you in this life
Makes you a woman;
I return you back to life
To live as such"

Cuando Casi Conocí a La Muerte

Flaquita,
La noche es tan oscura;
Me arrodillo ante usted
A la hora escogida;
Flaquita,
Consuéleme
Cuídeme
Cúreme
Quíteme

"No.

No, hija mía;
Siéntate ante mis pies huesudos,
Acuéstate bajo mi manto negro;
Te consuelo
Te cuido
Te curo
Pero no,
No te quito;

Lo que no te mata en esta vida
Te hace mujer;
Te devuelvo a la vida
Para que vivas como tal"

Coyoacán

The wrinkled brown man on the corner
Says he sells miracles;
      Good thing my pocket has a hole,
It must cost a lot
To make someone love you;

Coyoacán

El señor moreno arrugado de la esquina
Dice que se vende milagros;
      Menos mal que mi bolsillo tiene un hoyo,
Debe costar mucho
Hacer que alguien te ame;

A Pair of Catholic Knees

Perhaps in the next life
I will be a nun;
Be born old and stay old,
Wander covered in black,
Keep my head down and my mouth shut;
Live clean,
Live asexually,
Remain faithful to god with a blindfold;
Understand him,
Imitate him,
And feel p u r e for the first time,
If in this life I cannot be;

Un Par de Rodillas Católicas

Quizás en la próxima vida
Seré monja;
Nacer vieja y quedar vieja,
Andar cubierta de negro,
Mantener la cabeza baja y la boca cerrada;
Vivir limpia,
Vivir asexuada,
Mantenerme fiel a dios con una venda en los ojos;
Entenderlo,
Imitarlo,
Y sentirme p u r a por primera vez,
Si en esta vida no puedo ser;

Hospitality

Why ignore my demons
When I have a long wooden table and bread to
part in eighths,
When I have wine,
A warm home,
And a writer's block?

Eve

The first woman
And Motherless

You became
On cold and barren sod, alone and yet,
Beside your only captor;
You bled
For the first time, *confused*, alone and without
Another woman to teach you;
You sinned;
But Eve,
You were just a girl
Without a Mother
To tell you otherwise;

Aphrodite

From the loin of Aphrodite—
The birth
Of a single pomegranate;
    Creation;
    She held to her lips,
Then to the air
    A six-chambered eclipse
    To a soft and yellow sun;
Destruction!;
She crushed it
    Beneath her heel;
Pulp
    To now seedless soil;
    Sower; Creator; Destructor; and *GOD*
    Of
    Garnet-stained feet

To Sappho

Her hair,
Golden silk, violet-tressed,
Makes of me
A weaver;
My loom, too *eager,*
Runs itself bloody, through thorny vines
Whilst I hide behind this bush
To see her

Hester

Once scorned,
One could straddle
Sin and truth
On the scaffold
And in reprieve
Of indecision,
Be sorted
By man's iron finger

Homage to *The Scarlet Letter (1850)* by Nathaniel
Hawthorne

Dorothy

Pay no attention!
To believe in man
And his power
Is to kneel empty-handed
At the curtain
Of a lesser god

Homage to *The Wizard of Oz (1939)*

Rosemary & Her Baby

What is a woman
If not a contrarian to god?

What is a Mother,
If not a host to half
Of what makes a child ungodly?

Homage to *Rosemary's Baby (1967)* by Ira Levin

Sylvia

Faceless and bodiless
Pruner
At the crotch of my fig tree:
The rotten,
Now forgotten
Fig
Of willful departure,
Is no longer
For my picking

Dedicated to Sylvia Plath (1932-1963)

Friducha

Free, where?
>Prisoner,
>Free yourself!
Alive, in what life?
Dead woman,
Dig yourself up!

Preacher, to whom?
Deaf woman,
Listen to the sound of your own voice!

Dedicated to Frida Kahlo (1907-1954)

Friducha

¿Libre, por donde?
Prisionera,
¡Libérate!
¿Viva, en cúal vida?
Difunta,
¡Desentiérrate!

¿Predicadora, para quien?
Sorda nuestra,
¡Escucha el sonido de tu propia voz!

Dedicado a Frida Kahlo (1907-1954)

Pizarnik

And you,
Daughter of nobody and air,
I shouted at you like a Mother
When you looked over the living edge;

When you crossed it at last,
I saw—
That the old wind
Had given
An orphan
Her wings;

Dedicated to Alejandra Pizarnik (1936-1972)

Pizarnik

Y *tú*,
Hija de nadie y aire,
Te grité como Madre
Cuando miraste por el borde viviente;

Cuando lo cruzaste por fin,
Vi—
Que el viento viejo
Le había dado a
Una huérfana
Sus alas;

Dedicado a Alejandra Pizarnik (1936-1972)

The Tenth Muse

Tell me,
Has god given license to the poet to sin?

Ironic life,
I fell in love with the pen instead of a certain
person,
Although both
Would have made me
A sinner *{a poet}* in the end

Dedicated to Sor Juana Inés de la Cruz (1648-1695)

La Décima Musa

Dígame usted,
¿Dios le ha dado licencia al poeta para pecar?

Vida irónica,
Me enamoré de la pluma en vez de cierta
persona,
Aunque ambas
Me hubieran hecho
Pecadora *{poeta}* al fin

Dedicado a Sor Juana Inés de la Cruz (1648-1695)

Preface

Violent childbirth;

I *became* through an act of rage—

Now, I am seeded

With the

Mother

To

Morality; Below— an underworld,

Where my grandaughter

Has

Not

Yet

Been

Born:

Because of Our Culture

Because of our Culture—
We are at war;
This war,
Between Love and Culture,
Involves many soldiers;
In every home, every corner, every crevice, there is
at least one;
Loud-mouthed soldiers—
Those who only bark and shout;
"Dirty, sick, broken... devils, sinners, perverts" they
shout;
Armed soldiers—
Murderers with guns, illiterate religious people
with their bibles,
And parents with their conditional love;
Armed, are the murderers
Who hide behind the corner;
Armed, are the religious
Who god does not recognize,
Who 'cure' through acts of violence,
Who judge, who criticize,

And who cover their ears when god tells them
Not to judge or criticize;
Who use god's name to hide and justify their
prejudices,
And who will be left at the gates of heaven
For wasting their lives against another creation of
their lord;
Armed, are the parents
Who make their children orphans,
Who throw them out of the house to sleep on the
street,
Who are the empty chair at their child's wedding,
Who wanted children to raise identical copies of
themselves,
Who cry at the end of their lives because no one
visits them,
Who make their children choose
Between having parents or having a partner,
Culture or Love,
And who only regret doing so
When their child takes their own life;

And lastly—
The passive soldiers;
Those
Who out of habit, fight but do not know what for,
Who perpetuate the war with their silence,
Their complacency and their cowardice,
Those who are capable but blind;
...
For this, and for much more,
We are at war;
For this,
Our loving Culture does not love everyone;
For this,
I ask you—
To take off your uniform;

Por la Culpa de la Cultura

Por la culpa de la Cultura—
Estamos en guerra;
Esta guerra,
Entre el Amor y la Cultura,
Ocupa muchos soldados;
En cada casita, cada rincón, cada grieta, hay al
menos uno;
Soldados bocones—
Los que solo ladran y les gritan:
"Sucios, enfermos, diablos, pecadores, pervertidos,
rotos"
Soldados armados—
Los asesinos con pistolas, los religiosos analfabetos
con su biblia,
Y los padres con su amor condicional;
Armados, los asesinos
Que se esconden detrás de la esquina;
Armados, los religiosos
Que dios no reconoce,
Que los "curan" mediante actos de violencia,
Que juzgan, que critican,
Y que se tapan los oídos cuando dios les dijo
Que no juzgaran ni criticaran;
Que usan el nombre de dios para ocultar y
justificar sus prejuicios,
Y que se quedarán a las puertas del cielo

Por gastar su vida contra otra creación de su señor;
Armados, los padres
Que les hacen huérfanos a sus hijos,
Que los tiran de la casa para dormir en la calle,
Que son la silla vacía en la boda de su hijo,
Que querían niños para criar copias idénticas de sí
mismos,
Que lloran al final de su vida porque nadie viene a
visitarlos,
Que los hacen escoger
Entre tener padres o tener pareja, *Cultura o Amor*,
Y que sólo se arrepienten
Cuando su hijo se quita la vida;
Luego—
Los soldados pasivos;
Ellos
Que por costumbre, luchan pero no saben por qué,
Que perpetúan la guerra con su silencio, su
complacencia y su cobardía,
Los que son capaces pero ciegos;
...
Por esto, y por mucho más,
Estamos en guerra;
Por esto,
Nuestra Cultura tan amorosa no ama a todos;
Por esto,
Les pido—
Que se quiten el uniforme;

Lachesism

I cry out to the sky
To strike me;
Clouds, please part
And find me;
Womangod,
Be
A bearer of light— *Beam on me,*
     If I am
          True

I Am Out of Ink

I do not like sweet tamales
I do not like the state of the world
I do not like the illnesses of children
I do not like the genocide in Palestine;
I do not understand monarchy
I do not understand the height of the border
I do not understand why god makes my neighbor
suffer
I do not understand why innocent people suffer
the most;
I do not want anyone else with my last name to suffer;
I do not want to pay my debts
I do not want to shout
I do not want to love anyone who does not love
me; but,

But,
I want an epiphany
I want my rights
I want a big house with a balcony like in the
novelas
I want to publish a book, but,

But,
I am out of ink

Se Me Acabó la Tinta

No me gustan los tamales dulces
No me gusta el estado del mundo
No me gusta la enfermedad de los niños
No me gusta el genocidio en Palestina;
No entiendo la monarquía
No entiendo la altura de la frontera
No entiendo por qué dios hace sufrir a mi prójimo
No entiendo por qué la gente inocente es la que
más sufre;
No quiero que nadie más con mi apellido sufra;
No quiero pagar mis deudas
No quiero gritar
No quiero querer a nadie que no me quiera; pero,

Pero,
Quiero una epifanía
Quiero mis derechos
Quiero una casita con balcón como en las novelas
Quiero publicar un libro, pero,

Pero,
Se me acabó la tinta

My Disguise

What rose-colored life is this,
She, who wears a disguise?;
She
Who made of me a deer,
Useful; To make the wolf feel strong
Weak; With an inflicted canvas for a body
She
Who makes me skin the wolf
And wear his skin
To dodge her *a r r o w s;*

El Disfraz Mío

¿Cuál vida de rosa es ésta,
La que se lleva un disfraz?;
La cual
Me hizo venado,
Útil; Para que el lobo se sienta fuerte
Débil; Con cuerpo de lienzo infligido
La cual
Me hace pelar el lobo
Y ponerme su piel
Para esquivar sus *f l e c h a s;*

Ophelia

Beckoning!
I am a branch
About to break
Bottomless! Brooding!
I am the gaping mouth
Of the softest-raging river;
Can you resist me?

Homage to *Shakespeare's Hamlet (1623)*

Holden Caulfield

If I am to go to bed one night
      A *child,*
On the Eve of my becoming
      An adult,
Must Life and her scalpel
Seek me
For the removal of my spine?

I Have Never Tasted Coffee

I have never tasted coffee—
Not without burning my tongue;
I only ever get two slurps while it's scalding,
Stumbling into my first job;
After, and before my second job,
I get four to five more;
But by then, it is cold— a nasty layer of separated
milk sits on top; I toss it;
Sometimes,
People from class invite me to drink some,
I say no; I need the money to keep myself in school;
And other times,
The people I work for
Snap their fingers at me to serve them some during
their meetings;
But of course,
They never offer me any— *They probably know,*

I don't even know
What it tastes like

Written during my undergraduate at UCLA (2017)

Arachnophobia

There is an older man
Across the bar;
He encroaches
Like a spider spinning a fly into a web;
He tells me about himself,
His work, his money, his stocks, his cars,
Himself and more about himself;
His silk
Still spinning, he tells me
I am mature for my age; two decades and one year;
Suddenly— as I prepare for flight,
A tired-faced woman, unafraid of spiders,
approaches—
She lifts her shoe up high,
While a certain venom, some might have heard
before,
Leaks from the corners of his mouth:

"Honey, wait, I am so sorry"

The Thread

There must be a thread
Between us;
At least, between myself and the older woman
Who pretended to know me today,
When she noticed
A man was following me home;
I had not seen him,
But she did;
She made sure the man knew
She was watching me;
It was as if
She flicked her end,
Until my end
Began to rattle;
And then,
She did
What only an older woman,
Who has known the world longer than I,
Would know to do;
She used our thread
To pull me toward her
Into safety

Pavlov's Dog *{Bitch}*

A young man salivates:
An open-palmed, open-mouthed beggar of the
masculinity-granting body;
He starves, tugs on his leash, leaving his neck sore;
Drooling, whimpering, panting,
He sniffs and licks her footprints, till finally— she
feeds him;
Howling into the unvirgin night,
His stomach is full but his soul is e m p t y;

Where Are The Missing Women?

Woman,
Do not have a daughter so that you do not lose her
Mother,
Do not let her go out
My daughter,
Tell me when you arrive

My daughter—
My only daughter,

Have you arrived yet?
...

¿Dónde Están Las Desaparecidas?

Mujer,
No tengas hija para que no la pierdas
Madre,
No la dejes salir
Mija,
Dime cuando llegues

Mija—
Mi única hija,

¿Ya llegaste?
...

Child Mother

A girl,
Born to run,
Ran for her life
Down the only alley through which
They do not let *Our Virgin* pass;

Niña Madre

Una niña,
Nacida para correr,
Corrió por su vida
Por el único callejón por donde
No dejan que pase *Nuestra Virgencita*;

Date Night

'I should be enjoying myself'
     This is what I tell myself
But I cannot help but notice—
He chews with his mouth open;
The food
Ends up on his hands,
He smacks his lips, he licks
The grease from his fingers, ravenously, it reminds
me
Of a nature documentary—
A lion tearing open the body of a deer;
He legs
Are s p r e a d, mine are crossed, protecting
something;
His red, sweaty fists
Are gripped on the corners of the table;

He yanks
The table closer to him— I shudder; My appetite is
gone;
He strokes
The rim of my glass, and for a moment— I
question—
If my eyes missed something;
Later,
He takes me home—;
My lips are ready to tell him: *I enjoyed myself
tonight*
But I cannot help but notice—
His body
Blocking the door, is so much bigger than mine;
For a split second,
I wonder what I would yell if I needed to;
And if my neighbor were not home,
If anyone would even hear me;

Benightedness

The bluebird flying above
Does not realize
The world is upon destruction; Nor do some other
people I know;

The Empty Chair

I needed more
Than a plate full and a roof to keep out the rain;
  Never hungry; Never wet; I need(ed) you;
I did not need
A house of smoke, a missing seat or red stains from
empty bottles;
  Fed but hungry and housed but wet;
   Big, but small enough to still fit in your
    arms (*I need you still*)

Orphan I

Daughter of the country,
I am an orphan;
She— America, who I thought was a woman,
Has snipped me
From the umbilical cord,
Unwanted; Useless; Female,
In what has been
My second abandonment;

*Written as a high school student, the night of the 2016
election*

Orphan II

Daughter of wolves,
Today I am a sister;
My cave is a couch
For the unwanted, female fetus,
Abandoned like me,
By *Mother America*

Written as a therapist, the day after the 2024 election

The Cloth Mother

I am a baby:
I want warmth over the cold of metal,
A breast over a bottle,
A cushioned, soft core, a lullaby for a crier;
Why, hand to my chest, do I feel a wad of wire?

A Girl's Secret

Back before our feet hung off the bed, she had said:
There would never be a secret
Between best friends;
And so in the bed, where I pretended to sleep,
She lied awake and whispered
To me,
The secret
She knew
A best friend would keep;

...

I BELIEVE YOU

I believe you, I believe you, I believe you;
I believe you,
I b e l i e v e y o u ;
I believe you,
I believe you,
I believe you;
I.

Believe.

You.

Death Valley

'*Miles to go*'
A mirage
Makes my trail disappear;
Endlessness brown and red
From all sides,
It swallows me;
The dirt,
      Gritty, dry on the teeth;
A hawk— hovers and does not wing;
The heat,
Sweltering, stifling, and suddenly still; *Robert,*
      I can not see ahead of me

Homage to "*Stopping by Woods on a Snowy Evening*"
(1923) by Robert Frost

Not So Soon

Human, delicate animal, close your eyes;
Today we cannot trust,
And Tomorrow waits for you; Tomorrow tells me
She has a surprise— *everything you have ever wanted*
—

But Tomorrow says you must stay another day;

If you ever feel suicidal, you can text or call 988 to contact the Suicide and Crisis Lifeline or call the National Suicide Prevention Lifeline at 1-800-273-TALK (8255) to speak with someone. There is always someone to listen.

Adler

In the womb:
God,
Make me a leader!
Give me a stern face,
A demanding fist,
And a deafening voice!
Make me as strong as I can be!
In the flesh,
I was then sent to my family
As a first-born daughter

I Am Through With Fire

When I was sent to this world to be a woman—
I arrived with the idea
Of burning it to the ground;
I was born in a furnace, ablaze; I died ablaze, hot
but unscathed;

>And I will be born again *A Raven*—
>Tonight,
>Beneath my mantel

ON
THE HIGHEST
SELF

"It's a Woman!"

When the world began again—
As did I;
Reborn,
From the strike of lightning that killed me:
Where I laid,
A black and dusted silhouette
Of soot and ash
Reacquaint
The loose Earth with my remains, rising from
flame,
Like the birdwoman of the Morning;

Griffith's Observatory

Sirius,
Striking and concerned with your significance,
Me too;

But you have been seen! — and how does it feel to
be seen, Sirius?
How does it feel — to lay on the eye of the non-
believing while I
Have not had a single observer, *no, not yet;*

My Golden Birthday

As I write
I have just been startled awake
By impending age:
       Any blindfold
       Unmindful of foresight
       Has been unfastened from my eyes
       This morning;
As of now
The decade and myself are young;
And one day,
I may mourn this view from my bed—
Of the rest of my life
Laid out
Before me

Written the morning of my 25th birthday (2024)

Ego & Her Disrobing

Because
After one of the buttons came loose,
My finger, once a needle,
Instead
Disrobed me;

    Beneath
    This ill-fitting, second-hand disguise,
    My finger, in disbelief,
    Found a *WOMAN*, who in her nudity,
    is completely clothed

The Four-Leaf Clover of Faith

A patch of clovers grew
On the side of my childhood home,
Lush; green and unassuming

My father told me
There was a four-leaf clover
Somewhere in this patch,
        If only I searched for it;
I searched for it on reddened knees,
Kneeling on the female need
To gather;
Daily,
I gathered bundles of unluckiness,
Ripping them right from their roots, stubbornly as
I was,
Until there were no more clovers left to pick;

        I never did find the four-leaf clover
But still— I did not consider myself unlucky,
My luck,
Was simply, that while staring at a now barren
patch of soil,

I still believed I could find it;

The Violet Light

Two lights unite;
The deep blue of the night and the red of the
scorched sun;
A ray of violet
Ends the *Age of Ambivalence,*
And names me
The guardian of unity and doubled love;

La Luz Violeta

Dos luces se unen;

El azul profundo de la noche y el rojo del sol

quemado;

Un rayo de violeta

Acaba la *Era de la Ambivalencia,*

Y me nombra

La guardiana de la unidad y el amor duplicado;

Girlhood

I learned what a girl was
The day I fell from the branch of a tree;

Three older girls rushed over to me
Like Mothers:
The first girl
Took off her sweater
And tied a knot around my bleeding leg,
I hoped it was not her favorite;
The second girl
Took the rubber band out of her hair
And tied mine up;
She poured cool water onto the sleeve of her shirt
And pat the sweat off of my face;
She fed me water right from her bottle,
And although I was fainting,

Gasping and choking on my own tears,
I kept assuring her I did not have cooties;
The third girl
Who I remember the most
Was my protector;
She stood in front of me like a soldier,
Taller and more fierce than any girl I knew;
She fought off a group of boys
Who were trying to peak at me
And silenced those who were laughing;
She knelt down and held my reddened, tear-
streaked face
And smiled warmly—
She said to me, reassuringly, *"everyone falls
sometimes"*
And pointed to a scar
On her knee

FLIGHT

Family of soil, of salt, and the ground,
I was born the only bird;
I hear a wind whisper to me, words I understand,
I see the clouds part a path, wide and no one in way,
Family, *please*,
The wings of your daughter, your granddaughter,
Are poking out from her shoulder blades;

Written the night I was accepted into university (2017)

My GrandMother's Rosary

In the garden of my grandMother's home,
Bare feet in the grass,
It is 3 o'clock in the afternoon
And the sun sets on my skin;
I feel the hot and dry wind,
I smell maiz
And I see
The brown and rock-strewn range of mountains
As an outstretch of arms
That both embrace and entrap me;
I hear a rooster crow,
A dog howl
And the distant sound of her
Reciting the rosary—
The lasso that keeps me from floating away;

The Miracles

The foot
To open paths
The hand
To *create*, to touch what is tender
The eye
To see with intuition and protect from envy
The ear
To understand and discern the Truth
And the heart;
To shelter
The brothers; *pain and love*
So that they learn
To live together, in this house that feels

Los Milagros

El pie

Para abrir los caminos

La mano

Para *crear*, para tocar lo tierno

El ojo

Para ver con intuición y proteger de envidia

La oreja

Para comprender y discernir la Verdad

Y el corazón;

Para albergar

Los hermanitos; *el dolor y el amor*

Para que aprendan

Vivir juntitos, en esta casa que se siente

A Poet's Cast

I lived my entire childhood
Without ever breaking a bone;
I was timid
To ever jump from high places
As other children did,
Though I always wanted to wear a cast
As they did;

…

I suppose I wanted; I suppose I want
My wounds to be witnessed
Like any other animal;
I suppose I wrote; I suppose I write
To be beared witness to

My Privileged Pair of Eyes

If one should ask
Where to find the meaning of life:
Today, at least, it sat across from me;
On the blue couch, a beam of sunlight burst
through the blinds, casting itself on the floor of my
office like an epiphany of nature; this light then
set softly in the eyes of the person across from me,
making their tears stop and their life *begin*;

In the Margins of My Notes

Self,
Will I be a good
Therapist?
  How would I rate
  The intensity,
  Frequency,
  And duration
  Of the anxiety response
  Coinciding with
  This
  Thought?

Written while in a graduate school lecture (2021)

A Poem by My 7-Year-Old Self (2006)

I am something

Can you guess what I am?

I am something with pink shoes
I am something with a pencil
I am something with a name

I am someone

I am a girl

I AM AVA!!!

The Mirror

I wake before anyone else, my home is quiet and
a cast of dull, periwinkle light coats the inside,
leftover from the night;
I peak my head into each room,
My Mother and father are sleeping, my baby
brother rolls over in his crib;
Everything is as it was—
My books are where I left them, the scent of dry
wood in the air,
My old fish floating in his bowl;
I sit for a moment and breathe in the past, in my
lungs is where I keep it;
There is a creak in the floor — I gather my things
to go — Someone is waking up— I must hurry—
I look around only one more time —
But someone catches me there in the hallway—
it's *Little Me*
She gasps, so surprised to see me, I put my finger
over my lips,
        "Shhhhh...!" I say
Her pink blanket dragging behind her as she runs
into my arms,
I kiss her and wish her a good day at school,
Putting her down safely at the end of the hallway,
        "I'll be back to see you again, Ava"

THIS IS SHE

AFTERWORD

I have many to thank for the birth of this book. Thank you to the teachers who nicknamed me *'author'* in elementary school, to my colleagues who always remind me to dedicate time outside of work for writing, to my friends who have watched me grow up and endure the experiences I have written about, to my parents, brother and extended family who have never doubted me once, and once more, *to my grandparents*— to whom I owe my culture, language, and humility— I gift you my book.

EPÍLOGO

Tengo muchas personas a quienes agradecer por el nacimiento de este libro. Gracias a los maestros que me apodaron *'autora'* en la primaria, a mis colegas que siempre me recuerdan que debo de dedicar tiempo fuera del trabajo a escribir, a mis amigos que me han visto crecer y vivir experiencias sobres las que he escrito, a mis padres, mi hermano y mi familia extendida que nunca me han dudado, y una vez más, *a mis abuelitos*— a quienes debo mi cultura, mi idioma y mi humildad— les regalo mi libro.

ABOUT THE AUTHOR

Ava Cázares is a Mexican-American poet and licensed psychotherapist in Los Angeles, CA. Born and raised in Riverside, CA, she earned her Bachelor's of Arts in psychology and education from UCLA and her Master's of Science in Marriage & Family Therapy from USC. Now as a published author, she has acquired a second profession that makes others *feel*.

email: avamcazares@gmail.com
Instagram: avamadre